STEVE KING

THE MANAGER'S DILEMMA

A Manager's Guide to Change Management

THE MANAGER'S DILEMMA
A MANAGER'S GUIDE TO CHANGE MANAGEMENT

iUniverse books may be ordered through booksellers or by contacting:

iUniverse
1663 Liberty Drive
Bloomington, IN 47403
www.iuniverse.com
844-349-9409

ISBN: 978-1-6632-3202-1 (sc)
ISBN: 978-1-6632-3203-8 (e)

Library of Congress Control Number: 2021923288

Print information available on the last page.

iUniverse rev. date: 12/29/2021

Contents

The Manager's Dilemma

1

A few years back, I was talking with the CEO of a large organization. He was lamenting the fact that some of the key changes to the business he was hoping to implement had run into roadblocks. In a moment of frustration, he said to me, "I just can't get my frontline managers and their teams to get on board with the changes. Frontline managers … where my best ideas go to die."

I think he was looking to me for some validation of that sentiment. But I just raised my eyebrows and waited. After an uncomfortable moment, he went on to say, "I know what you're thinking. You're thinking I haven't prepared my managers for the change. Right?" He was right.

When I talk with managers, they often express their own version of frustration about change. They feel that leaders cook up changes, unleash these changes on the business, and then expect the manager to do all of the heavy lifting. That heavy lifting includes personally coming to terms with changes and then getting their teams on board as well.

We might call this the manager's dilemma. They are rightfully the leaders' representative on the front lines; so naturally, leaders expect managers to carry the change ball across the finish line. But managers might not even think the change is a good idea. That's a dilemma. Managers might not fully understand the what, why, and hows of the change they are supposed to execute. That's a dilemma. Managers might not be resourced to carry out the change. That's a dilemma.

Are managers helpless in this kind of situation? Are they set up to fail and disappoint? I don't think so. Even when senior leaders struggle to do their jobs as sponsors of change, there are plenty of things a manager can do to advance the change agenda and perhaps save the day. That is what this small book is—a tool kit for managers who are expected to make change happen.

Before we jump into the tool kit, I want to comment on change and senior leaders. It is commonplace to say change is the new normal. It never really lets up. When you talk with experts on change management, there are two conclusions they often share. First, most large-scale changes fail to meet expectations. Second, those failures have many causes, with poor leadership typically at the top of the list.

Why do senior leaders so often struggle to lead change? I have concluded that a lot of the struggle has to do with their presumptions. Here are a few common presumptions some leaders make: 1) people always adapt to change; 2) managers know how to manage change; 3) since the change is self-evident, everyone will get on board; 4) change just happens, and you don't have to manage it. These are myths or maybe half-truths. These presumptions keep leaders from rolling up their sleeves and getting to work themselves. These presumptions keep leaders from thoughtfully supplying managers with what is necessary to get their job done.

Returning to my friend, the CEO, and what he said to me—"I know what you're thinking. You're thinking I haven't prepared my managers for the change adequately. Right?" As mentioned earlier, he was right.

I didn't. But I offered to help. There are ways to prepare managers for their responsibilities in moments of change. And I am not talking about one specific change effort but any change that comes down the pike. In fact, that exchange between the CEO and me was one of the reasons I wrote this book.

What roles must managers play when change is bearing down on their teams? What change-management skills do managers need to successfully carry that ball across a finish line? How do they turn a leader's presumption that everyone knows how to manage change from a half-truth to a truth? If you want to know, read on.

Key Players in a Change Effort

2

Whenever a change is underway in an organization, there are probably four kinds of people playing a part in that change. First, there are sponsors of change. These are people with the power to decide if a change is going to happen or not. They typically have money and other resources at their disposal to fund the change. In the best of circumstances, they have accountability for the success or failure of the change.

Second, there are change agents. Change agents are like project managers. They have the task of actually making the change happen – what might be called "change implementation". When an organization is small, or when change is taking place in a smaller part of a bigger organization, the sponsor and the change agent might be the same person.

Third, there are advocates for change. These are people who have ideas for changes but no power or authority to make the change happen. They are people in search of a sponsor.

And finally, there are the targets of the change. These are the people who actually have to change in some way. They might be asked to use a new tool; follow a new policy; adjust to a new technology; work in a new space; or adapt to a new work process. In any case, targets of change have to modify their behavior in some way or another. Behavior modification is a common requirement for all change targets.

> Behavior modification is a common requirement for all change targets.

The following is an example with all four players on display.

Let's say that someone in a decent-sized manufacturing business, with twenty physical plants, decides it is a good idea to outsource plant security rather than employ their own security guards at each plant. They bring this idea to the vice president (VP) of plant operations, and the VP is persuaded. The VP checks with the CEO, who gives the OK to proceed. So far, we have met the sponsor of the change (the VP) and the advocate for the change (person with the original idea).

The VP tells the head of security she is responsible for making this change happen and to put together a plan. She reaches out to folks in HR, the finance department, and the legal department as well as three plant managers (one from a large plant, one from a medium-sized plant, and one from a small plant) to help her plan and implement this change. We have now met the first group of change agents. The head of security might be the lead change agent.

Once the plan is completed and the sponsor has signed off on it, it is time to implement the plan. At this point, the plan is shared with all twenty plant managers. Those twenty (actually seventeen) make up the second group of change agents, but they are different from the first. They were not in on the planning. They are simply being told to execute the plan. This is the manager group we are most interested in here in this book—change agents expected to move the change forward with little or no input to the change itself ... one source of our manager dilemma.

To keep these two different kinds of change agents straight, we'll call change agents in on the planning of the change the "primary change agents" and the change agents who were not part of the planning process the "secondary change agents."

To complete the change picture, who are the targets of this change? Certainly, the current security guards who will lose their jobs are targets of the change. I would argue that the head of security and the plant managers themselves are key targets of the change since dealing with an outsourced vendor will be different from dealing with their own security staff—including new processes and new behaviors for sure. Take note: those frontline plant managers are both the targets of the change and change agents ... another source of our manager dilemma.

So once again, four key players are found in most change efforts: sponsors, change agents, advocates, and targets of the change. We'll be referencing these four throughout the book.

The Manager's Responsibilities in a Change Effort—In a Nutshell

3

What will be expected of those plant managers in the previous chapter ... or in any change effort for that matter? What specific roles and responsibilities should a manager have to push forward a change agenda? I think there are three responsibilities: 1) communicator; 2) coach; and 3) advocate—all living under the umbrella of change agent or, more likely, secondary change agent.

Managers are essentially change agents. They represent the sponsors of the change, regardless of whether they agree with that change or not. Of course, a change agenda that makes sense to a manager is easier to cope with. But not all change makes sense at first blush to a manager. In chapter 5, we'll focus on how managers can come to grips with a change they disagree with or are uncomfortable with.

The bulk of this book is directed at exploring the responsibilities of communication, coaching, and advocating. To put it simply, managers need to effectively communicate the change to the team—repeatedly and clearly, over and over again. They need to continue to coach performance during the change. Managing performance and

> Managing performance and productivity is the primary job of a manager. It does not stop during change.

productivity is the primary job of a manager. It does not stop during change. But it may need to adjust during change. And finally, they may have to slide into an advocate role at some point during the change. Change plans rarely unfold exactly as planned. And who is in the best position to see change plans go off the rails? Frontline managers. When that happens, frontline managers need to be become advocates for adjustments to the plan. This means not only reporting what is going wrong but also suggesting what needs to be done to fix it.

So that CEO was right. His plans would continue to die with frontline managers unless those managers were properly enrolled in the change and trained/incented to communicate, coach, and advocate.

But before we jump into details about those roles, a thought about managing day in, day out team productivity while managing change.

The Productivity Dip

4

The manager's responsibility during a period of change is basically the same as it is during a period of calm and tranquility—to look after productivity and treat people with respect. Productivity during change is always at risk. This is why good change-management efforts should be casted as a risk-management exercise. Presumably, a change is an effort to improve or maintain productivity, so some might think that there would not be a downside. But there almost always is a short-term downside, and this downside is what managers are looking to mitigate by being good communicators, coaches, and advocates. I'm going to call this downside the *productivity dip.*

Let's imagine three kinds of productivity dips, each more profound or dangerous than the next. We'll call these mild, problematic, and fatal dips.

Well-managed changes include mild productivity dips. Change almost always requires that an employee's attention be drawn away from their regular work for a while … not a long time but just enough to cause a small, temporary productivity loss. There may be a short period of employee dissatisfaction and perhaps some resistance, but these pass, and things get back to a new normal on a reasonable timeline.

Some changes are so small and require so little change-management attention that this mild productivity loss is baked into the rollout. It's considered normal. For example, the rollout of Microsoft Office 365 might need a little communication and a little training, and the time needed to attend to these are minimal, so the impact on productivity is small. Larger or more systemic changes could be quite significant. Yet if the proper change-management efforts are applied to these bigger efforts, the same mild productivity dip should be expected. Mild productivity loss is a success for a manager, a change agent, the sponsor and, of course, the organization.

Problematic productivity dips have happy endings but are sad and difficult journeys. Problematic productivity dips are longer in duration and put at risk the goodwill of customers and employees. Consider this example. A company adopts a new inventory-management system. The goal is to more precisely manage inventory to control costs. Implementation of this new system requires a lot of change management. It includes not only a new technology but also new processes, new behaviors, and new metrics. Imagine the change agent team bungles the implementation. Say they attend to the new system requirements but ignore related and necessary process changes. The new inventory system goes live, and instantly there are issues. Frontline managers and their teams scramble to make things work. Workloads expand. Other work gets set aside in the frenzy to adjust processes to the new system. Some of the folks on the team who were excited about the new system become disillusioned. Worst ... some customers fail to receive shipments on time.

But let's say after some extraordinary efforts, things get back on track. Eventually, the new inventory system starts to perform as

> Problematic productivity dips have happy endings but are sad and difficult journeys.

expected. But unintended damage to productivity has been done. And perhaps there is a lingering reputation issue with customers and even employees.

Would this be a completely failed change effort? No, probably not. But would this be a suboptimized change effort with noticeable negative impact on productivity? Yes, probably.

By the way, notice who in this scenario receives the brunt of poor change management efforts: the frontline managers and their teams who are stuck trying to pick up the pieces of the mismanaged efforts. We'll come back to this in later chapters.

What is a fatal productivity dip? It is one where a change's expected benefits fail to materialize, and there is permanent damage to employee and/or customer relations. In our inventory systems example, imagine the system never performs as planned. Some customers get fed up with order delays and leave, and some employees get fed up with the added burden of working with a lousy inventory system and leave.

Can frontline managers really save a company from a fatal productivity dip? Probably not. This kind of extreme productivity issue was set in motion long before it arrived on the manager's doorstep. The best they can do is see the problems coming and advocate vigorously for changes to the implementation plan.

On the other hand, could a frontline manager gum up the works of a good implementation plan by failing to communicate, coach, and advocate? Could they turn a mild productivity dip into a problematic one? Yes, they could ... unless they were properly prepared to execute their responsibilities as communicator, coach, and advocate.

Managers Personally Coming to Terms with Change

5

In the story about outsourcing plant security, there were seventeen plant managers who had not been part of the planning process but were expected to carry out the change. What if some of them didn't like the change? What if they thought it was a bad idea to fire their security staff and use a bunch of strangers to do those jobs?

Before a manager can address their teams regarding a change, they first have to address their own feelings about a change. If the change is a welcomed one or a reasonable one, a manager will probably take a few moments to get on board and then turn their attention to their team. But if the manager has serious doubts about the proposed change, what should they do?

First, they can ask questions about the proposed change and see if, with a different perspective, more data, and time with others who have experienced similar change, they can get on board. Sometimes this is all it takes.

But sometimes that is not enough, and a manager remains concerned. If that is the case, the reluctant manager should share their concerns with sponsors and change agents. The sponsors and change agents might have missed something in the planning process—something that managers on the front line can see more clearly. The plan can be adjusted. And it is probably also good for sponsors to hear early on the kind of resistance they can expect to deal with in the rollout. Reluctant managers being candid are early warning signals of resistance to come.

There is a more personal reason for a manager to share any concerns they have. Many managers feel better about managing a change with their folks when they made the effort to send their concerns up the chain of command. At least they tried.

Let me acknowledge here that not all organizational cultures are open to managers providing upward feedback. In fact, some cultures might even punish managers who seem to be complaining about the upcoming change. So, do a realistic assessment of the risk of sharing concerns with the higher-ups. No need to push a boulder up the hill unless those at the top of the hill want that boulder ... well, maybe with one exception, which I will get to in a moment.

We have now arrived at another manager's dilemma. By virtue of being managers, there is a reasonable expectation that they will carry out the change effort as planned. They are expected to be team players, fulfilling their roles at the front line as representatives for the leaders of change.

But they might not support the change personally. What should they do? I think the answer is carry out the plan despite concerns. This may be a disappointing answer, so let me expand on it.

When someone signs up to be a manager, there are probably plenty of good reasons to do so—such as growing your skills, having a bigger impact on the business, helping others develop their skills, and making more money. Probably not on the top ten list of reasons was being the good soldier and carrying out someone else's agenda. But this is a fair expectation of the leaders who promoted you to manager. Most businesses are not a democracy, even if there is plenty of collaboration and opportunity to influence the business agenda. It's inevitable that at some point a manager will be asked to set aside their concerns and carry on. And it is a fair expectation of leadership. You know this is true because sometimes you have to do it yourself with your own team members who have concerns about your agenda.

> There are two ways to get on board with a change. One is to commit to it. The other is to comply with it.

There are two ways to get on board with a change. One is to commit to it. The other is to comply with it. These are two very different psychological frames of reference. Commitment suggests you're all in and you're all good. Compliance suggests you'll move forward despite doubts. No serious sponsor of change expects commitment from everyone. Realistic sponsors know that some will simply comply. As long as sponsors get a critical mass of commitment, they should be OK with compliance by the rest.

If a manager decides to comply, should they share their doubts with their team? Opinions differ on this. Some say yes; share any doubts about the change but leave no doubt the team will implement the change. Others say to keep the doubts to yourself and publicly support the leadership's decision. You'll have to choose the one most comfortable for you, which might change from situation to situation. When it was up to me, I typically shared my concerns and strived for compliance.

What if a manager finds themselves in a mode of perpetual compliance, with serious doubt about every change coming down the pike? I suspect this is a telltale sign that they are not a great fit with that particular organization. It would probably be exhausting to go to work, day in, day out, simply complying and rarely committing. That does not sound like a formula for workplace engagement, and we all deserve to be engaged in our work.

Finally, back to that exception about pushing a boulder up the hill to unreceptive leaders. If your doubts about a change are ethical or moral in nature, in good conscience, you have to express those concerns regardless of the consequence. Being party to a change that cuts against values you hold dearly will take its toll. If those kinds of concerns are not taken seriously, it might be time to plan your exit and go to a place that shares your values.

Communicating the First Mention

6

It has been said that change management has to do with three things: communication, communication, and communication. It might be more accurate to say that communication is a necessary part of a manager's role in a change effort, but not the only part.

What role does a frontline manager plan in a well-orchestrated communication plan for change? We can break that role into two parts. I will call part one *the first mention* and the second part *the rest of the story.* We'll get to the rest of the story in the next chapter. Here I want to focus on that preliminary announcement that change is on the way.

The goal in this announcement is twofold. First, it is to raise awareness about the impending change. The second is to harvest first reactions and questions from the team about the change.

Over dinner one evening, three change gurus offered me seven questions they thought the preliminary announcement should speak to. They felt that if a manager could reasonably and efficiently answer these questions with their team, they would be off to a good start, and I agree. Of course, in some cases, senior leadership would have already delivered messages about the change. So then the manager is simply repeating and/or expanding on leadership's message. In some situations, the rumor mill has already delivered the message, in which case the manager has the opportunity to validate and/or clarify the rumors.

Here are the seven questions:

1. What is the change?
2. How does the change fit into the overall business strategy?
3. What will the desired state look like when the change is over?
4. How stable will the desired state be? Will it remain constant or be subject to ongoing change?
5. How long will it take to reach the desired state?
6. What are the downsides of this change?
7. Whose behaviors will actually have to change as the result of this change effort, and what will those new behaviors be?

If you're curious about why these particular seven questions, take a look at the appendix of the book for more detail.

For any particular change effort, there might be an eighth or ninth question that needs attention. Sponsors, change agents, and managers should add a couple more to the list if necessary. But at minimum those seven questions need answers that the managers can then pass on to their teams. And they agreed that the answers should attempt to simplify the complex; these should not be long, drawn-out explanations.

Let's try out an example using a different outsourcing decision. Imagine a large, national manufacturing organization with fifty thousand employees, mostly hourly workers. The combination of organic growth and turnover requires hiring of about five thousand people annually. The decision is made to outsource the recruiting of all hourly employees to a third-party vendor. How might this change be described by a manager to a group of their managers, using this framework?

1. *What is the change?*

   The company has decided to outsource recruiting to an outside vendor. This means soon we will be working with this vendor to fill new hourly roles. The company will no longer have internal recruiters.

2. *How does the change fit into the overall business strategy?*

   We are making this change primarily as a cost-saving measure. Apparently, the company can save up to $200 per hire with this new arrangement, and given the amount of hiring we do, that comes out to a substantial savings. A secondary reason is that it is hard to keep up with new regulatory requirements related to recruiting, and an outsourced vendor is better positioned to be in the know since they keep up on behalf of many customers; it's their main and only business.

3. *What will the desired state look like when the change is over?*

   Instead of working with our current HR recruiter, we will be assigned a team of recruiters as our new partner. These recruiters will be housed off-site but accessible to work with managers on their hiring needs. Hiring managers will have access to a new technology that allows them to submit job requisitions, track applicant flow, and arrange/conduct interviews. Hiring managers will still have the final say on who gets hired. The new partner simply facilitates the process.

4. *How stable will the desired state be? Will it remain constant or be subject to ongoing change?*

We expect to negotiate something like a three-year contract with a new vendor, so once the contract is signed, we expect only modest changes to recruiting processes from time to time.

5. *How long will it take to reach the desired state?*

We expect this change to take about six months. Six months from now, the new partner will be in place and up and running.

6. *What are the downsides of this change?*

The most obvious one is that our current recruiters are going to lose their jobs. The company will ask that as many of them as possible be considered for roles with our new vendor, so some familiar faces may remain, albeit off-site. But we know this is a significant loss for those directly impacted—and a loss of some personal relationships for us. Secondly, with the new vendor, some processes we are used to will change, and some of us will have to adjust to these new processes.

7. *Whose behaviors will actually have to change as the result of this change effort, and what will those new behaviors be?*

The biggest behavior change will land on us as hiring managers. We'll have to get used to working with this new outsourced recruiting partner, which means getting used to a new technology and some new processes.

> Once the manager has delivered this first communication about the change, they should harvest the team's reactions and field any questions.

Where does a manager get the answers to these seven questions? From the sponsors of the change or their change agents. If the manager is lucky, all the information they need to answer the questions will be in sponsor and change agent communications. The manager simply repurposes the information for their team. If the sponsors and change agents have failed to provide enough information, then the manager should put on their advocacy hat and request clarification. One simple way to do this is to take these seven questions to the sponsors and change agents and ask how they would answer them.

Once the manager has delivered this first communication about the change, they should harvest the team's reactions and field any questions. These reactions and questions should be fed back to sponsors and change agents to help craft future communication. Sometimes this feedback loop can lead to adjustments to the change plan. Sometimes this feedback loop can foretell resistance to the change, which smart sponsors and change agents will want to know about, and the managers themselves may have to address it at some point. As we can see, managers should play integral and important roles early on in the communication process.

7

Communicating the Rest of the Story

After the first mention of the change, managers become a little like reporters. They communicate the what, when, and how of the change to their team as the change unfolds.

In the best of circumstances, change agents and sponsors communicate directly to employees about the change—up to and through implementation efforts. If those communications are effective, a manager needs only to check with the team to see if they have understood the communications and if there are any questions or observations. Just as earlier, if there are questions that a manager cannot answer, or if serious concerns surface, managers should pass these over to the change agents for a response. In this best-of-circumstances scenario, the manager is simply following up and ensuring the team understands what's coming.

Sometimes sponsors want to cascade ongoing information about the change rather than communicating directly with employees. Cascading in this context means executives ask their subordinates to communicate with their folks, who in turn communicate with their folks, and so on. In this case, the manager plays a bigger role—becoming the voice of the sponsor with their teams. To do this successfully, sponsors and change agents need to feed managers the talking points and the context around them. Again, when the talking points and context are clear, complete, and timely, a manager simply passes along the information and fields questions and observations.

There are two more difficult communication scenarios a manager might face. One is when cascading messages are incomplete and/or slow in coming. The other is when sponsors go altogether silent after the initial announcement. This is yet another manager dilemma. What should a manager do?

I think there are only two options available to a manager. The first is probably obvious: ask the sponsors for more information. Sponsors have a nasty habit of presuming that their first communication is all people need to get on board with the change. This is typically not true. So reminders from the front line that they would like more information can prompt sponsors to communicate more completely and more often.

The second option for managers is to imagine how the change will unfold, given the little bit of information available, and create some contingences for what appear to be the most likely change scenarios. Let's return to our recruiting outsourcing example. Say the manager who delivered the first mention of the change hears nothing else. She only has answers to those seven questions. With only that information in hand, here are two contingencies she might put in place. First, she might try to staff up fully, anticipating that when the switch to the vendor takes place, there will be lag time (productivity dip) in hiring as the new vendor gets up to speed. Second, she might do some forecasting of future hiring needs so that when the new vendor arrives, she can address immediate hiring needs and fill the hiring pipeline with future hiring needs right away. Managers who can build a few contingency plans with only a little information are probably going to fare better in a change moment than those managers who simply throw up their hands and wait for what will happen next.

CHAPTER

Coaching the Emotional Responses

8

Change can be an emotional experience. Something familiar is ending, and something unfamiliar is beginning. This transitional moment often requires a manager to take off their communications hat and put on their coaching hat.

What's the difference between the two hats? The communicator is sharing information and harvesting reactions. The coach is trying to help someone struggling with their reactions.

People occasionally react to changes in a way similar to how they react to death. You might have heard of Kubler-Ross's stages of grief: denial; anger; bargaining; depression; acceptance. There are plenty of similarly staged transition models for change. You'll find many of them with a quick web search. Here is a simple one that could describe what your employees will go through: 1) awareness; 2) worry; 3) experimentation; 4) acceptance.

The manager as communicator raises awareness and understands those worries. The manager as coach addresses those worries and encourages experimentation.

There is an acronym that's sometimes associated with managing people through these kinds of change transitions—a WIFM. WIFM stands for "What's in it for me?" It is popular in change-management literature to suggest that if you want to get someone on board with a change, you have to address what's in it for them. I generally agree. I think there are two kinds of WIFMs. One is the informational WIFM, and the other is the emotional WIFM. For some of us, simply having the right information about a change is good enough. The information contains enough perspective on the change that I see the WIFM and I can commit or comply without much more. The emotional WIFM is an entirely different thing. Some changes strike an emotional chord for team members, and often those emotions are the basis for resistance to the change. When resistance is rooted in emotions, the manager should see their role pivot to coach rather than communicator.

> When resistance is rooted in emotions, the manager should see their role pivot to coach rather than communicator.

When faced with any emotional response to a change, your first coaching task it to acknowledge the person's concern with respect and seek to understand their worry. This simple step is essential to opening a pathway to experimentation and acceptance. If you already have a trusting relationship with your staff member, this step will be easier. If you do not have that trusting relationship, this step may take a while. Either way, you have to take it. Here are some questions/comments you might use when faced with an emotional response to the announcement of a change.

1. "Can you walk me through how you are feeling about the change?" (Don't ask what they *think*; focus on how they *feel*.)

2. "Can you help me understand why you feel this way?" (Is the change taking something away from them that they care

about? Or placing something in front of them they fear? Or is it something else?)

3. "These feelings are reasonable and understandable worries. I've had similar feelings about previous changes myself. Not now, but maybe in our next conversation, you could share with me what might make you more comfortable with this change." (Affirm the feelings. Affirm you can relate to those feelings— but for heaven's sake, don't go on and on about yourself. Honor the moment by not trying to fix the feelings in that moment. Instead, lay track toward experimentation in a later conversation.)

A word of caution. Coaching is different from counselling. All of us bring emotional baggage to the workplace, and sometimes a workplace change can trigger those emotions. Managers should not hold themselves responsible for addressing the deeper psychological wounds of others. If those wounds present themselves to a manager, a sympathetic ear is warranted, but playing psychologist is not. With permission from an employee, it is not passing the buck to bring HR into the picture, letting them work with someone who is exceptionally disturbed by a presenting change.

And one final word about change that is in fact dangerous to the livelihood of your staff. There are situations where a change results in people losing their jobs or reorganizing work into jobs that are boring or distasteful. The adoption of new automation, for example, can have this result. When this is the case, it's always best to treat people like adults and be honest with them. Earlier, I suggested seven questions best addressed when starting to communicate about a change. One of those questions was about the downside of the change. That is where this honestly belongs and begins. Hopefully, an honest organization will have contingencies for those at risk that managers can lean into, like stay bonuses, severance, and outplacement services.

In some organizations, sponsors refuse to speak with honesty about the ramifications of their change agenda. To call this a manager's dilemma might be understating the word *dilemma*. It places managers in an untenable position since most employees can see the handwriting on the wall, even if the sponsors are pretending the writing is not there. Managers who find themselves in this situation need to put on that advocacy hat and lobby for straight talk from change agents and sponsors, as well as support for employees impacted negatively by the change. It is simply the right thing to do.

Some More (Wise) Advice on Managing Resistance

9

I decided to write this book because I felt there was not much literature out there to specifically help frontline managers manage change. But as I am sure you know, there is plenty of literature out there about change management from just about every other perspective.

One of the finest and most respected researchers and writers on change management is John Kotter, Harvard professor and founder of Kotter International. I love his work and recommend just about anything he has written on the subject of change.

But one of his books (cowritten with Lorne Whitehead), *Buy-In: Saving Your Good Idea from Getting Shot Down*, has particular relevance for frontline managers. It presents a story centered around a change facing the fictitious Centerville Library. The story is illustrative and fun to read. But it is the second part of the book they call "The Method" that is particularly valuable to managers.

In that section of the book, Kotter and Whitehead outline twenty-four common forms of resistance people will throw out there to challenge a proposed change. Kotter and Whitehead suggest some good ways to respond to each of those twenty-four challenges. Of course, there are more than twenty-four barriers people can throw at changes they do not like. But these twenty-four seem to cover the most common territory pretty well.

I recommend getting a copy of *Buy-In*. Any attempt by me to summarize these twenty-four barriers and responses would not do the book justice, so I am not going to try. But I do want to give you a little taste of just one of those twenty-four to whet your appetite and encourage you to learn about the other twenty-three.

I have chosen #1 on their list. The statement of resistance sounds like this: "We've been successful, so why change?

This, of course, is a very shrewd form of resistance since it offers simultaneously a compliment (we're successful) with a rationale for not changing (we're successful). I can very easily imagine a team meeting where a manager introduces a change, and someone on the team says, "Why bother to rock the boat? We're already doing great." In fact, I may have said something like that one or two times in my career.

If a manager suspects this statement is rooted in a strong emotional response to the change, then the kind of coaching we explored in chapter 7 might make sense. But if the manager suspects this statement is simply a fact from the team's point of view—not an emotional response but more of a cognitive response—then the manager can offer some other perspectives.

In *Buy-In*, Kotter and Whitehead advise the manager to point out that adaptability to changing situations is the key to long-term success. For example, Disney was quite successful at full-length animated motion pictures. Why change and get into the theme park business? Netflix was doing pretty well sending movies to people's homes. Why bother to get into the streaming business? These are big-picture examples. There are simple and relatable examples as well. My hard drive works just fine. Why store things on the cloud? I can go to the store to buy that. Why bother ordering it to be delivered? We know there are sound reasons for all of these changes. And those reasons have to do with adapting to some threat or opportunity. Those reasons just needed an airing.

The answers to this "We've been successful, so why change?" question should be available in the manager's first-mention communication—in the answers to the seven questions a manager uses to introduce a change to the team. This is where the message of adaptability and the counterpoint to "Why change if you're successful?" can be found. This should be the reference point for the manager's response. Explain the logic of the change and why success often builds on success.

Kotter and Whitehead also advise managers not to turn the discussion into a debate or be dragged into a point-by-point analysis of a fifty-two-page business case. A fierce debate suggests the resistance is more emotional than cognitive, and a different kind of coaching is needed. And remember, in the end, the unconvinced still have the option to simply comply rather than commit. And in some change moments, that might be good enough.

> A fierce debate suggests the resistance is more emotional than cognitive, and a different kind of coaching is needed.

Kotter and Whitehead take on twenty-three other common statements of resistance and suggest strategies to respond. I suggest you get a copy of *Buy-In* and build up your inventory of responses for when the resistance comes your way.

Coaching to Change
Tendencies and Proclivities

10

There is an exercise I sometimes use in a classroom where I ask teams to imagine they can change McDonald's in any way they'd like to make it more profitable. What changes do they propose? Team report-outs seem to fall between two ends of a spectrum. One end of the spectrum I'll call the *incremental* change path to profitability. These incrementalists want only to tinker with McDonald's' traditional formula for success. They might offer a bigger individual serving of fries. They might offer some new meal deals. They might bring back loveable McDonald characters (remember Grimace?).

The other end of the spectrum I'll call the *revolutionary* path to profitability. The revolutionists are not interested in traditions or the current structure. They suggest McDonald's is entirely out of step with current market realities and recommend wholesale changes to the menu (for example, all vegan); a complete overhaul of the store decor (think big, stuffed chairs and fireplaces); and getting rid of those golden arches as a market message that the old McDonald's is no more.

Of course, there are shades of gray in between incrementalists and revolutionaries. But I am sure you get the point. All of us have a tendency or proclivity when it comes to change. Managers will have their own natural orientation; team members will have theirs. Managers will have to address both ends of this spectrum while perhaps sitting near one end of that spectrum themselves.

These tendencies are not emotional reactions. Instead, they represent preferences that the manager needs to take into account as they communicate and coach.

Incrementalists prefer the known to the unknown. They like to improve effectiveness by more efficiently utilizing existing resources. They prefer change that is gradual and incremental.

Revolutionaries are comfortable with the unknown and speculative. They prefer a faster, more radical approach to change. They like to improve effectiveness by upsetting the status quo.

Once again, all of us are capable of reacting to a particular change in either of these ways. I can look back at my career and see that I was an incrementalist in one situation and a revolutionary in the next. But most of the time, I suppose I leaned toward revolutionary. That was my proclivity.

Why is understanding these distinctions of value to managers? Because managers are likely to have to address both tendencies on their team, as well as their own tendencies.

Let me use this moment to put a plug in for diversity of thought. If everyone on one of my teams leaned revolutionary, I might not be appropriately challenged by incrementalists, who would be advocates for a slowed-down, moderated approach to a change. Sometimes those alternative incremental points of view appropriately challenged me to reconsider. Thank goodness they were on my team!

Of course, this book is focused largely on change imposed on managers and their teams from somewhere else in the organization.

The change path or trajectory has been set, and the manager and team members are likely reacting in one of two ways. How can a manager address these alternative reactions?

In our earlier example of the new outsourced arrangement for security at plants, the change was pretty big. The seventeen plant managers who were not in on the planning certainly would have had some kind of reaction the first time they heard about the change. Since it was a reasonably big change, those leaning toward revolution might have been fine. The big change suited them. The incrementalists might have needed their boss to help them understand this change. In this case, the company's head of security (the boss) might have started with the details of the change, not the big picture. Details give incrementalists assurance that the change is well planned and will be

> Incrementalists and revolutionaries have unique needs in moments of change, which a manager can address with a little forethought and insight into the tendencies that exist on their team.

well managed. The boss might ask incrementalists what specifically they need to know about the change and then go get that information. This gives incrementalists an outlet to express their concerns and gives the boss the opportunity to alleviate those concerns in follow-up conversations.

Incrementalists and revolutionaries have unique needs in moments of change, which a manager can address with a little forethought and insight into the tendencies that exist on their team.

If you'd like to get more than just a casual take (or guess) on your team's comfort with change (and your comfort as well), I suggest you consider a team exercise using an assessment tool called Change Style Indicator. This assessment is a little more sophisticated than the binary choices of incremental and revolutionary I outlined here. It's a great tool for naming team proclivities and predicting reactions to change.

11

Coaching Performance during Change

We have spent the previous few chapters focusing on how a manager can help coach reluctant staff through a change. That orientation deserved the real estate I devoted to it because most managers worry about change resistance from their own team members.

But we should not forget that through any change, a manager is still responsible for ensuring the continuation of quality productivity. The manager needs to continue to be a performance coach.

In my book *Six Conversations*, I introduced six conversations a manager and their employees need to have on a regular basis to ensure solid performance and engagement. Those six conversations are casted as questions regularly asked by employees. Those questions are as follows:

1. What is expected of me?
2. What and how should I develop?
3. How am I doing?
4. How did I do?
5. How will I be rewarded?
6. What is next for me?

What about during periods of change—particularly disruptive change? Do these six questions still matter? The answer is yes, of course they do. But the manager needs to reframe these questions a bit to make them relevant to the change that's afoot.

Let's go back to the earlier example of the introduction of a new inventory system. And let's say that introduction is going well. The new technology is working, related processes and behaviors were well defined, and the productivity dip was mild. This success was likely supported by a manager adjusting the six conversations in the following ways to keep her crew productive:

> Regularly collaborating with the staff around these adjusted six questions allows a manager to keep performance moving in the right direction

1.   What is expected of me as we switch over to the new inventory system?

2.   What new skills will I need to use this inventory system, and how do I get those skills?

3.   How am I doing adapting to the new inventory system?

4.   How did I do adapting to the new inventory system?

5.   How will I be rewarded for adapting to the new inventory system?

6.   Because of my mastery of this new inventory system, what might be next for me?

Regularly collaborating with the staff around these adjusted six questions allows a manager to keep performance moving in the right direction as the change agenda also moves along.

That example of managing performance was particular to the introduction of a new inventory system. But it can work for any change you encounter. Here is the generic version for when a change is being introduced:

1. What is expected of me during this period of change?
2. What and how should I develop as the result of this change?
3. How am I doing with this change?
4. How did I do with this change?
5. How will I be rewarded as I adapt to this change?
6. What could be next for me because of this change?

Let's do a quick overview of the rationale for these small adjustments to the six conversations in a change scenario.

What is expected of me during this period of change?

Change is rarely introduced into an environment without some new performance expectation of someone. For example, if a dental clinic purchases technology for creating crowns within minutes in the office, there will be new performance expectations of the dentists and their assistants to use that technology. Managers should be specific about new performance expectations related to the change.

What and how should I develop as the result of this change?

Change often requires a new skill or behavior for someone. In this example, the dentists and their assistants in the clinic will need to learn how to use the new technology. Perhaps some will be eager to do so. Perhaps some will be reluctant. Either way, the manager will need to ensure the learning happens.

How am I doing with this change? How did I do with this change?

These, of course, are questions about performance feedback in the face of the change. As the change is being implemented, employees will want to know that they are on the right track. In our dental clinic, the manager might arrange for a rep from the company that builds and sells the new technology to sit in on the first five uses of that technology and give feedback as the procedure is taking place. This addresses the "How am I doing with this change?" question. Additionally, the manager may have the same rep meet with all of the dentists and dental assistants after all have used the technology a few times to offer some observations and field questions. This addresses the "How did I do with this change?" question.

How will I be rewarded as I adapt to this change?

It is unlikely that frontline managers and their staff will see direct monetary rewards for their part in making a change successful. Maybe in rare occasions, bonus money is handed out as a thank you, but in my experience, that's unusual. However, there are other kinds of rewards a manager can wield. Personal recognition for extra effort and celebrations at key milestones are certainly available to most managers as reward mechanisms. If the change results in advancing personal portfolio skill sets (résumés) or the freedom to handle a job with more autonomy, then a manager should be explicit about these kinds of intrinsic rewards with their staff. Certainly, all of these nonmonetary rewards are at the fingertips of the manager of that dental clinic.

What is next for me because of this change?

Of the six conversations, adjusting this one to a particular change is admittedly a bit of a stretch. "What's next for me?" is basically a career conversation, so if a change happens to bring about a new career opportunity, great. A manager should certainly leverage that. But it would probably be happenstance. For example, maybe one of the dentists at this clinic has the ambition of opening their own office someday—an ambition that they have shared with the manager of the clinic. That manager might discuss with them the value of mastering this new technology as part of their career plan.

Beyond these six conversations, there are plenty of other things a manager can do to ensure the staff maintains and even improves performance during a period of change. But tending to these six in the fashion I have outlined here is a very good start.

Retention during Significant Change

12

Earlier in this book, we highlighted the inevitable productivity dip that accompanies change. Mild productivity dips are to be expected and generally are manageable. But problematic and fatal productivity dips should be a particular concern since some employees may take troublesome change rollouts as a cue for their departure. They may see bad change management as an indicator that their job is in jeopardy. They may see bad change management as an indicator that senior management is leading the organization poorly. Or they may simply find the change itself one they cannot even comply with, let alone commit to.

One scenario a manager does not want to find themselves in is that surprise moment when your best performer walks into your office and says, "I'm leaving." If a manager has been having that "What's next for me?" conversation on a regular basis, that surprise moment is less likely to happen, since the next career move has been talked about. But a big change might prompt someone to make a premature exit. How can a manager avoid that moment?

The answer is called a *stay*

> A stay conversation is a check-in as a change is picking up steam to find out how an employee is feeling about things.

conversation. A stay conversation is a check-in as a change is picking up steam to find out how an employee is feeling about things. It is not a complicated conversation. It is probably as simple as these questions and observations:

1. How are you feeling about the change?
2. Is there anything particular I can do to help you with this change?
3. Let me share with you (reiterate) the value you bring to our organization. Here are some specifics …
4. Let me share with you my thoughts about your future in our organization.

Notice this is not a pitch to the employee to stay. It is not a sell job. Instead, it is an honest conversation about how the employee feels about the change, their job, their future, and the organization. Again, if a manager has been regularly having those six conversations and coaching to / communicating about the change well, this stay conversation might be a little redundant. But that is OK. Better safe than sorry, right? And of course, if the employee shares doubts and concerns, the manager would then have an opportunity to right that ship.

Perhaps the more awkward aspect of a stay conversation is who you choose to have it with. Some managers have a pecking order in their head. Their high potentials and those key to making the change happen absolutely get a stay conversation. What about those who are solid performers and regularly meet expectations? What about poor performers? What about staff members who the manager suspects will not succeed after the change is implemented?

I know some managers who used a big change as a reason to let a poor performer go. I don't care for that approach (or should I say excuse) for terminating an employee. If someone is a poor performer, they deserve the following things: they deserve feedback about their poor performance and they deserve the opportunity to improve and some help doing so. And if things don't work out, they deserve to be treated with respect and dignity as they exit the organization. That is good management. A change itself should not be used as an excuse to dismiss.

What if a manager fears that someone on their team will not be able to make the necessary adjustments to succeed in a changed environment? Here is a real example a friend of mine recently faced. He ran a project management office (PMO). His project managers were tapped to lead major initiatives within his organization. Those initiatives ranged from installations of new systems to orchestrating facility and office moves. As time passed, more and more of these projects carried a large technology component. This was the slow-moving change facing the PMO. An IT background become a critical competency for his staff.

It turned out that one member of his team had virtually no IT experience. For a while, he was able to give her work that required very little technology acumen. But that work dried up. If the solution in this case was to simply help the employee get the necessary technical skills quickly, he would have gone that route. But the learning curve was too steep. This was not an option.

Time for a "stay or exit" conversation. Perhaps there were other roles within his group or in the organization she was qualified for. She might be offered one of these jobs. In fact, there were a few roles like that, but they were roles with less responsibility and lower pay. She declined. And with that decline, the conversation turned to an exit conversation, which was managed with respect, acknowledgment of the good work she had accomplished, and outplacement help.

The simple truth is sometimes change claims innocent victims.

The Manager's Role as Advocate

13

In the first chapter of this book, I suggested there were three responsibilities managers must take on when change comes from on high: communicator, coach, and advocate. I have touched several times on one aspect of that advocate role—addressing an existing change plan.

As a change plan unfolds and things do not quite go as planned, frontline managers can certainly play the reporter, letting change agents and sponsors know what is going on. This is not exactly advocating. Advocating is offering a solution to a plan gone awry. Or it might even be more proactive than that. It might be offering suggestions to a proposed plan that seems clearly flawed.

> Successful advocates seem to share one characteristic. They are skilled influencers.

As I mentioned earlier, there are some organizations where sponsors and change agents don't welcome bad news or differing points of view. Advocating in those environments is risky, and managers should proceed with caution.

How should managers approach sponsors and change agents with feedback and recommendations for adjusting plans? Successful advocates seem to share one characteristic. They are skilled influencers. They can successfully make a case for change either directly to sponsors or to others who can influence sponsors.

These influence skills are a complex array of interconnected competencies, skills, knowledge sets, and behaviors. But here are three aspects of influence skills that have stood out to me as I have watched skilled advocates do their thing.

Data. They have the facts. They have the data. They know how to present it in compelling ways. The best advocates I have seen present a balanced collection of data. They include data that supports their argument for change and data that acknowledges the downsides of the proposed change. They let that information then speak for itself. For example, I have seen technology leaders share data on compliance risk that convinced senior leaders to fund new technologies (even though there was countervailing data presented by those same technology leaders acknowledging the new spend would add little to productivity targets).

Experiences. Often advocates have personal experiences related to the change that sponsors do not have. They share these experiences as education devices, giving sponsors another point of view. For example, I have seen diversity, equity, and inclusion officers, who are diverse themselves, share personal experiences with senior leaders that opened their eyes and paved the path to thoughtful diversity and inclusion efforts.

Assumptions and beliefs. Smart advocates are astute about any assumptions or beliefs they carry into their arguments for change. Assumptions and beliefs are opinions, perhaps rooted in a little data and a few experiences, but they are primarily subjective. Thoughtful advocates catalogue their assumptions and beliefs and willingly share them with potential sponsors. When they find sponsor assumptions and beliefs in sync with theirs, the path to successful advocacy is easier. When they are not in sync, the path gets bumpy, and the weight of influencing sponsors falls back on gathering more data and expanding the pool of persuasive experiences. For example, I have seen divisional business leaders convince senior management to fund a new product line with few facts but convincing assumptions that seemed to tap into senior management's core beliefs.

Advocates play such an important role in the change process. And the leveraged use of data, experiences, assumptions, and beliefs are part of those advocates' tool kit of influence. So whenever I talk with groups about the players in the change game, I elevate advocates from "featured player" status to "starring role" on the marquee. I always put them on equal footing with sponsors, change agents, and targets.

There is one more dimension to advocacy I want to comment on before I wrap up on the subject. Everything in this chapter and other comments about advocacy throughout the book speak to managers reacting to change plans—plans either in motion or proposed. But managers might have their own change agenda in mind. Perhaps they see the opportunity to adapt a new technology or improve a process or alter a cultural norm as a means of improving performance, productivity, and engagement. If those changes can be made within the confines of their own team, they're probably free to proceed. But if those possible changes go beyond their team borders, they will need some sponsorship to make things happen.

In this circumstance, their advocacy is *for* a change, not *about* a change. They are advocates in search of a sponsor. And when they think they have found that sponsor, they will need to bring to bear key data, experiences, assumptions, and beliefs mentioned a moment ago to influence that sponsor to take up the cause. They might even lay out their argument using the seven questions covered in chapter 6 (the chapter devoted to the first-mention communication strategy).

Some very fine managers have bought themselves recognition and regard being that kind of advocate.

14

Final Thoughts

There are so many things that go into successful organizational change efforts; I don't want to oversell the role managers play in those efforts. But ignoring their role in these kinds of efforts is a mistake. Our lamenting CEO from the first chapter grew to understand this.

It takes lots of shoulders to lean into change work, and in most organizations, there are more manager shoulders than C-suite shoulders. Once managers know their roles in change efforts and get skilled up on some basic communication, coaching, and advocacy competencies, they can and probably will be one of the key success factors.

One final thought about managers and change. Once a change effort is completed and business resumes, who is likely to oversee this new normal? In most cases, it is managers. Managers are often the guardians of change legacy. They sustain the change.

I have read plenty of change-management books that are long on advice to sponsors and change agents on how to start and implement change but short on advice on how to sustain it. Look no further than the pool of managers for sustaining a change effort. They are the foot soldiers of change.

Appendix

Why These Seven Questions?

In chapter 6, I introduced seven questions a manager should be able to answer for their teams at the inception of an organizational change. These were questions I picked up from change-management gurus. Those questions are as follows:

1. What is the change?
2. How does the change fit into the overall business strategy?
3. What will the desired state look like when the change is over?
4. How stable will the desired state be? Will it remain constant or be subject to ongoing change?
5. How long will it take to reach the desired state?
6. What are the downsides of this change?
7. Whose behaviors will actually have to change as the result of this change effort, and what will those new behaviors be?

Why did the gurus want frontline managers to answer these particular questions at the first mention of a change (acknowledging that eighth and ninth questions might be added for a particular change)? Here was their thinking.

Question #1 is obvious. The manager needs to name the change as clearly and concisely as possible. This is the headline.

Question #2 answers the *why* question. At minimum, the rationale should be tied to a business goal. The appearance of change for change's sake needs to be nipped in the bud from the get-go. Tying the change to a business goal does that. Team members might be doubtful that the change will improve or protect the business goal. Or they might think there are better ways to achieve the business goal. These signs of resistance are important for the manager to capture and then give as feedback to sponsors and change agents. So offering up an answer to this question helps flush out resistance and create clarity.

I have seen managers go a step further with this second question. Some external event might have prompted the change. Helping the team see the relationship between the external event and the change can sometimes help speed up acceptance. The pandemic starting in 2020 is an obvious example of an event that prompted plenty of change. Often, the external event is more subtle. In chapter 6, I used the example of outsourcing recruiting and the rationale of cost savings as the reason why. Cost savings is a business goal. But the recruiting industry had seen a decade of improvements to recruiting technologies that made outsourcing a recruiting function a viable, cost-saving option. So including that external event in the answer to question #2 might add some additional punch to the explanation.

Question #3 is simply a more detailed version of question #1. The first question is the headline. The third question is the story associated with the headline. Since this is the first mention of the change, the story here should be a short story, not a novel. Managers should leave details about the future to later communications. Here, they should focus on giving the team a sense of what it will be like to live in the changed world and how it will be different from what is happening now. This gives the team an image to ponder. They can decide if they like or dislike that image.

Question #4 speaks to the issue of change fatigue. Since change is omnipresent, people get tired of one change piling up on top of another change. So as a kind of heads-up, question #4 gives the team a sense of whether this change is one and done or if they should expect it to unfold in waves. People can manage the fatigue better if they are given this heads-up.

Question #5 can also prepare for the fatigue factor, but its primary purpose is to help the team with planning for distractions. If the answer to this question is "Big change is on its way, and the process is going to unfold over the next two weeks," then everyone knows considerable distraction from daily routines is on its way. If the answer to this question is "Big change is on its way, and the process will unfold over the next two years," then everyone knows distractions from daily routines will come in fits and starts. Either way, they can begin to mentally plan accordingly.

Question # 6 is the "let's treat everyone here like an adult" question. It is the rare change that does not have a downside for someone in the organization. Too often, sponsors are so excited about their change they fail to acknowledge any pain that change might cause. This failure breeds cynicism, which can sabotage the change itself. Perhaps worse, cynicism as an outcome of poorly managed change breeds negative cultural norms that negatively impact performance long after a particular change has come and gone. This question is intended to acknowledge the downside while also suggesting the downside is necessary to achieve the positive, expected outcome from the change. Again, people can disagree with this balance. But at least the answered question gives an outlet for that disagreement to surface.

Question #7 speaks directly to the targets of the change and one key danger of any change effort—placing too much emphasis on changes to process, technology, structure, or metrics and too little emphasis on the behavior change required. Changing a process or a metric is much easier than changing a behavior. People are more complex than work diagrams and work standards. This last question names the most dangerous pitfall to a change right up front in the first mention of the change. Smart managers will keep the answer ever present throughout the change effort.

About the Author

Steve King is the retired executive director for the Center for Professional and Executive Development at the University of Wisconsin's School of Business and the president of SDK Group, which specializes in helping organizations find solutions for their business-related talent-management issues.

Steve teaches at the University of Wisconsin–Madison, Northwestern University, and Morehouse College in Atlanta.

Steve spent more than twenty-five years leading in corporate settings. He was the senior vice president of human resources for Hewitt Associates, a global HR consulting and outsourcing firm. He also served as the vice president of global talent management for Baxter Healthcare; faculty leader for the Bank of Montreal's Institute for Learning in Toronto; and vice president of management and professional development for Harris Bank in Chicago.

Steve lives in Madison, Wisconsin, and is the author of four other books on management: *Brag, Worry, Wonder, Bet*; *Six Conversations*; *Alignment, Process, Relationships*; and *Prevention and Contingencies.*

Recommended Reading

Clearly, since I spent an entire chapter plugging it, I recommend:

> John Kotter and Lorne Whitehead. *Buy In: Saving Your Good Idea From Getting Shot Down.* Harvard Business Review Press, 2010.

If you are looking for a nice overview of organizational change management, I would recommend:

> Rebecca Potts and Jeanenne LaMarsh. *Master Change, Maximize Success.* Chronicle Books, 2004.

I touched on the skill of influence as I worked through the manager's role as advocate. If you are looking for a more robust understanding of what it takes to be an effective influencer, I recommend:

> Susan Finerty. *Master the Matrix.* Independently published, 2012.

I mentioned an assessment tool that I think is an excellent way to surface change tendencies and proclivities. That assessment is titled *Change Style Indicator* and is provided through Discovery Learning International.

I referenced some of my own earlier work in this book. If you would like to go deeper into the six conversations, you should consider reading:

Steve King. *Six Conversations.* iUniverse, 2015.

And if you want to learn more about the use of data, experience, assumptions, and beliefs when influencing others consider reading:

Steve King. *Prevention and Contingences.* iUniverse, 2020.

And my other two books for managers are pretty good as well:

Steve King. *Brag, Worry, Wonder, Bet.* iUniverse, 2013.
Steve King. *Alignment, Process, Relationships.* iUniverse, 2019.

'

Made in the USA
Las Vegas, NV
15 March 2022